101 THINGS

every couple should have done at least once

A kiss on The Eiffel Tower

What at first glance seems like a cliché is still a romantic gesture with memorable value. A kiss on the Eiffel Tower in Paris can be the crowning glory of a visit to the city of love.

Done

2

Taking a dance course

There is a reason why dance in films is the original form of passion. With a dance course together you don't just pursue a hobby, but maybe you find a whole new fire for your own relationship.

Photo shooting with a professional

Memories are still best captured in photographs today. Going to a professional not only provides inspiration for the shooting, but also guarantees that the photos will still be a pleasant memory of the time spent together for many years to come.

Organizing a dinner for friends

A good relationship also always lives through contact with mutual friends. A dinner in the living room at home not only promotes friendship. The joint organization and execution of such a dinner evening is a challenge that welds together and revitalizes the common chemistry for partnership.

Visiting a Theatre

The theatre is the typical symbol of cultural entertainment. But it is above all a way to break out of the known world, to make yourself pretty and to experience an unforgettable evening. And maybe you will enjoy the theatre and find a new hobby together.

Done

Hosting a games evening

Board games are on the rise again. Especially in times when most people are only on the move with their mobile phones, playing together at the table is a great way to experience communication in the old way and have fun together with your partner or friends.

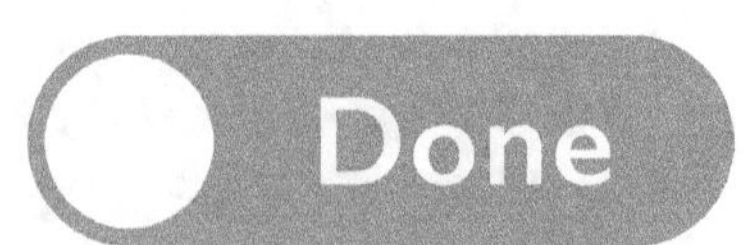

Writing a love letter

There are feelings that are simply difficult to express with the spoken word. The love letter allows a longer look into one's own soul life and is a very special proof of affection for the partner.

Relive the first date

How did you meet? Where did it all start? Would you do anything differently? These questions can easily be answered by rearranging the first date. If you remember the roots of your first acquaintance, you might rediscover old and especially appreciated sides of your partner.

Finding a common sport

Joint activities are one of the keys to a long and successful relationship. Doing sports together would be a great way to spend your free evenings while doing something for your body and health.

Planning a world Trip

Even if you do not have the money for the trip, planning a trip is an interesting insight into the desires of your partner. Who knows, maybe at another time the plan will be taken out of the drawer again and will be the basis for an actual trip around the world.

11

Set up a flat Together

The furnishing of one's own home is a factor for a harmonious living together. You can plan and choose the furniture and wallpaper of your own apartment together and thus create a common nest for a good time.

Visit a sex shop

Of course, being together in bed is also important for a good relationship. A visit to a sex shop is spicy, but may offer the odd stimulus for preferences or for new techniques that can enrich the relationship life anew.

13

A wellness weekend Together

Especially when both partners find themselves in a difficult and demanding job, relaxation is important for living happily. A visit to a wellness weekend together is an intensive time and offers many opportunities for beautiful and relaxing memories.

Making a drink Together

Nowadays it is no longer difficult to create a cocktail yourself. Based on the tastes of both partners, you will try your way through the different possibilities and in the end you will find a drink that is exclusively for you and your partner.

A holiday in a lonely hut

Switch off and leave the various influences of everyday life behind. Nowhere does this work better than in a lonely hut - whether in a forest, in the mountains or on a beach. Here you get to know each other anew and enjoy a time together without any disturbing noise.

16

A tandem jump out of the plane

If you are not afraid of heights, you should take part in this adventure. Jumping out of the plane together is a unique experience and in this form will certainly be something to tell your friends about.

Done

A long walk through nature

Spending time together in nature is a good key to having fun and simply spending quality time together. Why not leave everything behind and explore the surrounding nature on a walk?

A cooking course

Love goes through the stomach. That's no longer a secret. Of course, this works even better if you find favourite foods together or learn new ways of cooking. This possibility is offered, for example, in a joint cooking course.

19

Watching a series

Today there are many high quality series that can entertain for whole days. A series is something to look forward to in the evening and just the right basis to snuggle up together.

Shopping at the weekly market

For time together, it does not always have to be far away. Even a trip to the weekly market together offers many new impulses and influences and, last but not least, conversation that can fill entire evenings.

A Trip To Venice

Besides Paris, the city of Venice is considered one of the most famous destinations for couples travelling. The city, with its many canals and gondolas, is considered one of the most romantic destinations in the world. You should have seen this for yourself.

A gondola ride

The possibility of a gondola ride through the canals of Venice - or any other city - is surely one of the most romantic things one can do as a couple. Guided only by a gondolier, you can let the magic of a city work its magic on you and enjoy the time together.

Cooking Together

Often in the stressful everyday life the home kitchen is too often ignored. Instead of leaving the hot plates cold, you should arrange one day a week to choose a dish together and prepare it together.

Filing Tax returns Together

Of course, hardly anything is as little associated with romance and passion as the tax return. But a relationship also requires that you have to be an adult. The tax return brings with it stress and conflicts. Once you have gone through this, you grow even closer together.

Hosting a Christmas party for the family

Christmas is the right time to get into a contemplative mood together with friends and family. Of course, organising a Christmas party in your own four walls involves a lot of effort. It is rewarded with happy memories and happy faces around the table.

Develop a common passion for collecting

Collecting is one of the most interesting hobbies of all. It leads to flea markets, remote corners and joint researches in search of the missing pieces. A shared passion for collecting is a great way to spend your free time.

A visit To the flea market

Flea markets have a charm of their own that is difficult to describe. But one thing is for sure, a walk together is just as refreshing as the one or the other find, which you can acquire here for your own home or hobby after long and tough negotiations.

A visit To Ikea

The Swedish furniture store is the first stop for furnishing, decoration and new ideas. One would be surprised how quickly many hours pass in the aisles and shelves from the short trip in search of a new bin.

29

A road Trip Through The USA

Hardly any other country has as many different corners, charms and sights as the United States. A road trip through the different states creates common memories that will last a lifetime.

Attaching a lock to a bridge

The shared castle on a bridge symbolises the eternal love between a couple. In addition, they can return to the place together and remember the moment when they manifested the eternal love together here.

Getting a common pet

A pet is a great solution for all those who want to have another life in their own four walls. Whether dog, cat or rabbit - the jointly cared for and looked after living creature is a great way to complement the partnership.

Find a favourite restaurant

For joint excursions in the evening or on weekends it does not always have to be adventurous. If you explore the restaurants in your area, you are sure to find a place that will become the most popular destination for joint culinary ventures.

A visit to the zoo

A visit to the zoo is not only a great way to spend time together. The zoos combine a completely natural charm and especially with an annual ticket it is a great way to spend time together in nature.

Organizing a dinner for the parents

The blessing of the parents also plays a role in the success of the relationship. A joint dinner for all participants is a great opportunity for exchange and offers new impulses for the partnership.

Attending a wedding Together

The wedding of friends and relatives is not only a nice option to meet friends and relatives. Maybe you will find the one or other impulse to find some ideas for the most beautiful days in life yourself.

Keeping a "New Year's resolution" Together

The good resolution is as much a part of the turn of the year as fireworks and Feuerzangenbowle. How about simply choosing a common resolution that you can break in the first few days instead of just being disappointed by your own resolutions?

Watch an erotic film

Sex plays an important role in a relationship and especially in a stressful everyday life and a long time together, it is sometimes difficult to maintain this aspect in the right way. Perhaps watching a spicy film together will bring new impulses for your own love life.

38

Painting Easter eggs Together

Painting Easter eggs is a fun and varied idea in the spring of every year. Together you can give free rein to your creativity and enjoy the results later on by hiding the eggs for your partner anywhere in the house and garden.

Making a visit to Amsterdam

The city of Amsterdam attracts not only with its canals and its many sights, but also with a relaxed atmosphere. If you ever have the opportunity to visit the city with your partner, you should definitely use this option for a holiday together.

By bike through Amsterdam

The bicycle is the Dutchman's favourite means of transport. Together with your partner you can become part of the crowd, explore the many canals and small streets and explore Amsterdam in the most original way.

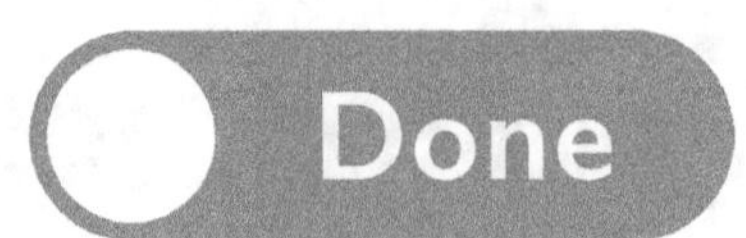

Visiting a folk festival

Folk festivals of various kinds can be found almost everywhere. Maybe you even manage to surprise your partner when throwing cans or shooting. Of course, the obligatory visit on the Ferris wheel is a must.

Once stranded together in the distance

What is a horror for tourists is a challenge for every couple. If you are completely without a navigation system, you will have to work together to find the right destination in the end.

A visit to the museum

Art and culture are a great way to spend your free time together. Why not let the works in a museum have an effect on you and in this way develop the conversation material for many evenings together? Moreover, the diversity of museums is inviting for common interests.

44

Visiting a concert

Music plays an important role in many areas. It is also an important part of life in many relationships. You should take the opportunity to go to a concert together and enjoy the music of the artists you love together.

45

Learning a new language Together

The world continues to grow closer together and language skills are as much in demand today at work as they are in leisure time. However, learning a new language from the very beginning is tedious. Together, the efforts become much more enjoyable and success is sure to follow.

Strolling Through New York City

New York City is a city with many charms and things to discover. For many people a trip to the city is an unfulfilled dream. One should fulfill this dream together and discover the many things this city has to offer.

Buy underwear for your partner together

Pretty underwear not only stimulates the attraction to the partner but also makes the wearer feel better. It can be very interesting to let your partner decide what your loved one should wear underneath.

Visit a wedding fair

A trade fair for weddings is not only interesting for couples who are planning their way together. It is a great insight into another world and offers many opportunities for fun together on a free weekend. And maybe you will find inspiration for your own celebration.

Pick an animal in an animal shelter

In an animal shelter many small animals are waiting to find a new and above all loving owner. Even those couples who have not yet planned to take an animal into their home will surely find a lovely piece of jewelry that they would like to have in their own four walls.

Working together in the garden in spring

Just like in spring the plants are blooming, the time begins when you have to take care of the appearance. Working together in the garden is a beautiful and varied way to spend time together and pursue a hobby.

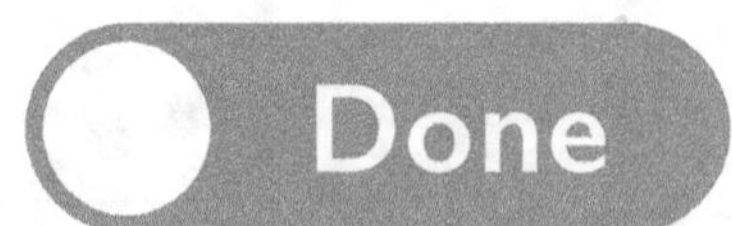

Create a common song list on the Internet

Today, the services in the network allow the creation of various playlists for different purposes. It is therefore very easy to create a list of the most popular songs and access it at any time.

52

Play the lottery together

Whoever plays the lottery together not only has the opportunity to win a high prize. With every cross on the slip of paper you can dream a little and imagine together with your partner what you would spend the main prize on. A great hobby with the chance of a high prize.

53

Visiting The Stadium

Visiting a stadium or a sports event is a nice activity that can be done especially in the big cities. Maybe you will discover a new hobby or just enjoy the time together while you remember the hustle and bustle on the field.

Carving the names on a Tree

Love wants to be held for eternity. A classic, which is already recorded in old books, is to carve your own name into the bark of a tree. If a particularly beautiful specimen can be found during a walk together, the opportunity should be taken to immortalise it together.

Doing a good deed together

Doing good deeds together not only gives the couple a good feeling, but is also a service to society. By helping out in an association or doing voluntary work, the partners find something that gives them time together and the feeling of having done something good.

56

Watch a Thriller Together

Cuddling together on the couch and watching a thriller is a nice activity for a Sunday evening. During thrilling scenes you simply move closer together to better endure the excitement.

Visit an All You Can Eat restaurant

Many restaurants offer the possibility to simply stuff your belly and feast until there is no tomorrow. If you have to support each other to end up back on the sofa at home, you know you had a great time together.

Once by Train Through the city

The exploration of the common homeland should be just as important as the striving for the distant future. Once you have drawn a map for local transport, you can simply let yourself drift through the many stations and perhaps discover one or two corners of your own city that have not been on the radar before.

Optimize the application documents of the partner

Especially the resume needs regular updates. Four eyes see more than two eyes. So why not sit down on a cold Sunday and review and optimize your partner's documents together? After all, the money from professional activities is the basis for life together.

60

Signing the partner's plaster cast

Once a minor or major injury occurs, this opportunity should be used in the best possible way. Such a cast is a nice memory of a rather questionable time. It becomes even better if you can find your partner's signature on your plaster cast.

Buying a gingerbread heart

Every folk festival offers many interesting opportunities for couples. One of the classics of a visit should be to treat yourself to one of the kitschy gingerbread hearts, which have equally sugary sayings on them.

Drinking a beer together at the Oktoberfest

So that one does not slide off the bench during the visit to the Oktoberfest, one should pay attention to the beer consumption. Instead of getting lost in the big beer glasses, it is a nice thing to share the first measure at the festival.

The kiss into the new year

If you want to check off the list of things that a couple should have done once, the obligatory Hollywood kiss at midnight of the new year should not be missing, of course. It is a proof of affection that comes from every cliché, but is still a very romantic gesture.

Done

Reading a book Together

Books offer a magic that most people appreciate. Instead of simply reading next to each other, it makes sense to read together. One can choose a common title and in this way find not only occupation but also interesting material for conversation.

Planting a Tree

Your own partnership should also find one or the other symbol that it is created for eternity. Planting a tree together is only one of the many options. Again and again, you can watch it grow upwards and represent your own relationship.

Done

Join a club

The common club can be the shooting club, a sports club or an activity that deals with political matters. This activity offers a new option of how to spend time together and find an approach to how common passions are born.

67

Going on a demonstration

Of course, many couples also have strong similarities in political and social terms. There is hardly anything that unites and merges you as much as a joint visit to a demonstration to make clear which topics are important in your own life.

Doing the spring cleaning

Just when the weather is getting warmer, the new blossoms can be seen in the garden and you yourself are awakening from spiritual hibernation, time is actively to be found. The sins of winter are washed away and together you bring the basis of your own relationship back to an acceptable level.

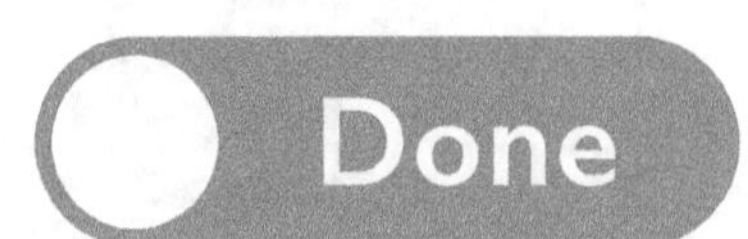

Swimming together in a lake

A visit to the swimming pool is a good option. It is even more interesting to stop during an excursion and simply take a bath in a lake and enjoy this activity in nature.

Shower Together on Sunday morning

A shower together is not only particularly intimate, it also connects partners in many different ways. Especially the morning on Sunday is a good time to take time for each other and to go into the shower together to show your partner affection in such an intimate way.

Experience a "blind dinner" Together

The blind dinner robs us of our senses and is therefore already an interesting experience. Of course, it only gets even better if you share this experience and memory with your partner.

Set up a piece of furniture from Ikea

The instructions from the Swedish furniture store are a challenge. It becomes easier if you do this together with your partner and in this way not only create a piece of furniture together for the apartment or house, but also get annoyed together about possible mistakes.

Baking a cake Together

Sweets are known to be the source for the release of happiness hormones. A cake is not only the right approach; by doing something together, you learn a little and can enjoy creating a delicious cake or pie together.

Ice skating Together

A visit to the ice rink or to the frozen pond are nice opportunities for a joint activity. If both partners are not so far at the stand as far as balance is concerned, common laughter is almost guaranteed as soon as the first falls happen.

Climbing a mountain Together

Active couples in particular should set themselves goals. It doesn't have to be Mount Everest, but climbing a mountain is a challenge that can weld together and provide a whole new impulse for the relationship and the success that comes with it.

Take a bike Tour

The joint tour on a bike is a great way to explore the environment and spend the weekend together. In addition, exercise is a good way for the partners to spend more time together anyway.

Swimming in the sea together once

For many people, the sea is synonymous with a call to the distance. If you ever have the opportunity, you should simply grab your partner and pull him or her into the waves, so that together you can answer this distant call by taking a bath in the salt water.

Looking for a common godchild in a poor country

Charity is a good thing and is also an interesting approach for most relationships. The exchange with the sponsored child is not only a good thing, it also offers a lot of interesting information about foreign countries and destinies that should be explored.

A visit to a couple therapist

A therapist does not necessarily have to be consulted if something does not go as expected. The professional in matters of relationships can provide interesting new impulses and prevent. Maybe you will find interesting new approaches for your own life and for the relationship.

Visiting the drive-in cinema

For many years the drive-in cinema had disappeared from the scene. Nowadays, this classic form of entertainment is becoming more popular again. A visit to the drive-in cinema combines the memory of the past with the shared memory of a great activity.

Done

Dancing Swing in a nightclub

For many years, swing was the expression at all when it came to pleasure. Even today, there is still the possibility to follow this special dance in the cities, not only having fun together with your partner, but also impressing the other guests with your own dance arts.

Having a picnic together in the park

A picnic is a romantic way of spending time together in nature. Delicious food and entertainment is a great way to get another point done, which is presented in many movies in Hollywood.

Have a pyjama party like Teenagers

The memory of childhood is a little bit wistful, especially in the later years. Why not take the opportunity to go back to this time? The pyjama party with your partner is an interesting option and can awaken memories from childhood.

Done

84

Making a staring contest

Who blinks first? Who gives in first? Competitions with the partner bring a very special fire into the relationship. The staring contest can take place at the breakfast table or simply at any place and is a humorous activity that you should have experienced with your partner.

85

Have a eating contest

And in the end you can even give yourself a title for it! Best Pasta Eater, Queen of Hot Dogs or Emperor of Burgers. Be a child again and find out who gets more in his stomach without surrendering directly.

Pretending to be strangers in a bar

Another cliché from the movies that offers an interesting impulse from reality. If you get to know your partner in a bar in a completely new way, you will not only have an interesting impulse for the relationship, but you are also facing an interesting adventure.

Making a film as an eternal memory

The Internet has changed the shape of memories. But if you make a film about a special adventure or just about life together, you still have an eternal memory of a wonderful time spent together.

Go to a wine tasting

Wine is a great cultural and above all culinary complement. Since it is not always easy to recognise the many differences in the types of wine, a joint visit to a tasting is a great activity for couples.

Buy a star

The possibility of naming a star after yourself is probably one of the most romantic options available. One look at the sky and perhaps you will discover the sparkle that is symbolic of the shared connection.

Visit a karaoke bar

Just be silly for once. There is hardly any place where this is as successful as in a bar where exactly this is on the programme. Here you will find many opportunities to live out together and sing the song that stands for the relationship.

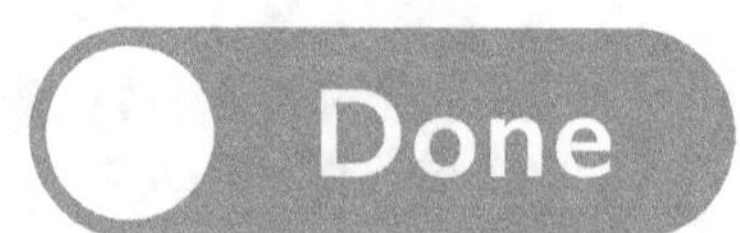

Done

Making Sushi Together

Sushi is a craft that needs to be learned. But you can certainly embark on the common adventure of making the fresh rolls in your own household. This is an activity that requires tact and cooperation.

Painting each other

This activity does not even require great artistic skill. Actually, the will is more important than the actual execution. And in this way a unique memory is created with absolute certainty.

Done

Take a spontaneous last minute vacation

Just pack your things, go to the airport and take the trip that is available. Such an adventure is certainly connected with great memories and shows the spontaneity in your own relationship.

Looking at the stars together

Sometimes it is important to leave the fast pace of life around you aside and focus on your own person or relationship. This hardly works better than the moment when you lie down in the damp grass and watch the stars move above your head.

Living on a farm for a weekend

Back to nature: this is the topic when couples decide to simply spend a weekend on a farm. This return to our roots is a great activity together and offers a glimpse into a completely different time.

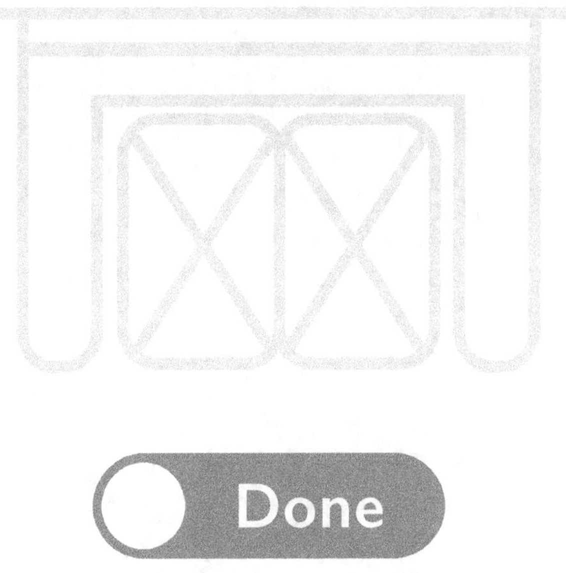

Done

Camping in the nature

It can also be interesting to do without the hotel and to reflect a little more on nature. With little more than a tent and a few supplies, you go out into nature and experience a night in complete seclusion together with your partner.

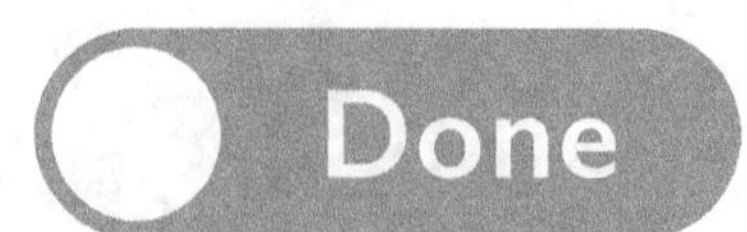

Attend a crime dinner Together

It is not without reason that crime dinners have become so popular in recent years. Maybe you spontaneously become an extra in history yourself and have a lot to tell yourself about this visit at the end of the evening.

Watching a horror film

Getting scared together is not only a great excuse for cuddling up during a movie, but also offers a great and exciting evening. Important: Clarify beforehand what kind of horror you want it to be, so that it doesn't turn into a really unpleasant evening for one partner.

Hire horses and ride on the beach

Of course, this is once again a typical scene that is suggested to us in movies. But why shouldn't we actually experience this? It's a little dream that can be realized with simple means.

Visit Romeo & Juliet's balcony

The visit of Romeo and Juliet's balcony in Verona is a cultural piece of history. Perhaps you will find your own story, even if it is far less dramatic than the original.

Done

Getting Married

Whoever has done all these things and got through them together with their partner should really no longer hesitate to take the last step together. Walking down the aisle is not necessarily the last step - but it is the crowning glory of the shared affection, time and community that has developed over the years.

Done

Publisher: © 2017 Selbstimpuls, ANGRON GmbH, Würmstr. 55, 82166 Gräfelfing, Germany

www.ingramcontent.com/pod-product-compliance
Lightning Source LLC
LaVergne TN
LVHW041335200726
843509LV00009B/730